ALL THE CATS IN THE WORLD

Sonia Levitin

ALL THE CATS IN THE WORLD

ILLUSTRATED BY
Charles Robinson

HARCOURT BRACE JOVANOVICH, PUBLISHERS

NEW YORK AND LONDON

by the same author
JASON AND THE MONEY TREE
A SOUND TO REMEMBER
THE NO-RETURN TRAIL
NOBODY STOLE THE PIE

For my mother who, when we were poor, still fed the hungry...

Text copyright © 1982 by Sonia Levitin
Illustrations copyright © 1982 by Charles Robinson
All rights reserved. No part of this publication may be reproduced or transmitted in any form or by any means, electronic or mechanical, including photocopy, recording, or any information storage and retrieval system, without permission in writing from the publisher.

Requests for permission to make copies of any part of the work should be mailed to: Permissions, Harcourt Brace Jovanovich, Publishers, 757 Third Avenue, New York, New York 10017.

LIBRARY OF CONGRESS CATALOGING IN PUBLICATION DATA
Levitin, Sonia, 1934- . All the cats in the world.
SUMMARY: An old woman is taunted by the lighthouse keeper for feeding the abandoned cats that live near the lighthouse, but when she falls ill, he has a change of heart.
[1. Friendship—Fiction. 2. Cats—Fiction]
I. Robinson, Charles, 1931- ill. II. Title.
PZ7.L58Al   [E]   81-20036
ISBN 0-15-202396-8   AACR2

B C D E   FIRST EDITION

Printed in the United States of America

Down by the seaside, among the rugged rocks and cliffs and in the shadow of an old lighthouse, lived many, many cats of different kinds and different colors. All were wild. They howled in the night.

Some had been left by thoughtless people. Others had strayed from their homes. Many had been born right at the water's edge, so this was the only home they had ever known.

The cats lived together among the rocks, watching the tides and the gulls and searching for food.

Now, it happened that some time ago two old women, noticing the cats, began to feed them. Soon they came every morning, just after dawn, with sacks full of food—liver scraps, fish heads, and bread crusts. The two women, Nella and Mikila, were good friends. They willingly shared the burden of feeding the cats, for although they were poor, they cared about hungry creatures.

The old women were still quite nimble and strong. They would clamber down among the rocks, calling, making certain that every cat got its share. They had named all of them.

"Ah, Mittens, and there is Puff. Here is your breakfast, little Tabby. Good morning, Tiger and Freckles and Spots."

After each cat had eaten and licked its whiskers and paws, up the rocky path the women climbed, slower now, and hot from the morning sun, talking as good friends do.

One day poor Nella died, and Mikila was left all alone. She wept bitterly. She went to the church to pray.

Late in the afternoon she remembered the cats. She had not fed the cats!

Weary and sad as she was, Mikila got up and hurried to the fishmonger, the butcher, and the grocer, and for a few pennies she gathered the scraps for her cats.

She arrived at the cliffs panting and out of breath, partly from hurrying, partly from weeping.

When the cats saw Mikila, they emerged from behind the rocks meowing, their tails held high. "Where were you?" they seemed to say reproachfully. "We were hungry. Why did you fail us?"

"I did not fail you, my little ones," Mikila said, as though they had really spoken. "Our friend, Nella, is no more on this earth. But do not fear. You will not go hungry. As long as there is a breath in Mikila's body, you will have food to eat."

The cats leaped and roved from side to side, and some even came to rub against her legs.

Suddenly Mikila heard gruff laughter. She looked about, startled. Partway up the slope, on a long, flat rock, a bearded old man sat looking down at her.

"Woman!" he called. "What are you doing with that sack of food?"

"I am feeding the cats," shouted Mikila. "What does it look like to you?"

"It looks like a foolish woman," replied the man rudely, "meddling where she does not belong."

"I belong here as well as you!" retorted Mikila.

"I belong here well enough," called the man, "for I am keeper of the lighthouse."

"Then keep your lighthouse," shouted Mikila, "and leave me alone."

Still the old man watched. By and by he called down, more curious than rude, "Woman, pray tell me, are you so rich that you can afford to feed fine morsels to these filthy creatures?"

Mikila retorted, "I manage with a few pennies a day, buying leftovers from the stores. Is it any business of yours?"

The old man muttered, "It is a shame to waste good food on cats."

Angrily Mikila left, determined to bring even more scraps tomorrow. She would show that old man—what did she care that he thought her foolish?

The next day Mikila waited purposely until afternoon. Her sack was heavy as she went down to the sea, calling, "Tina! Bennie and Spots! Here Tabby, Minnie, and Ruff."

Again she heard harsh laughter from up on the ledge.

"Old woman!" the man called down. "Aren't you afraid, at your age, to climb those rocks? You could fall and break your legs!"

"I'm not afraid!" She laughed and thumbed her nose at him.

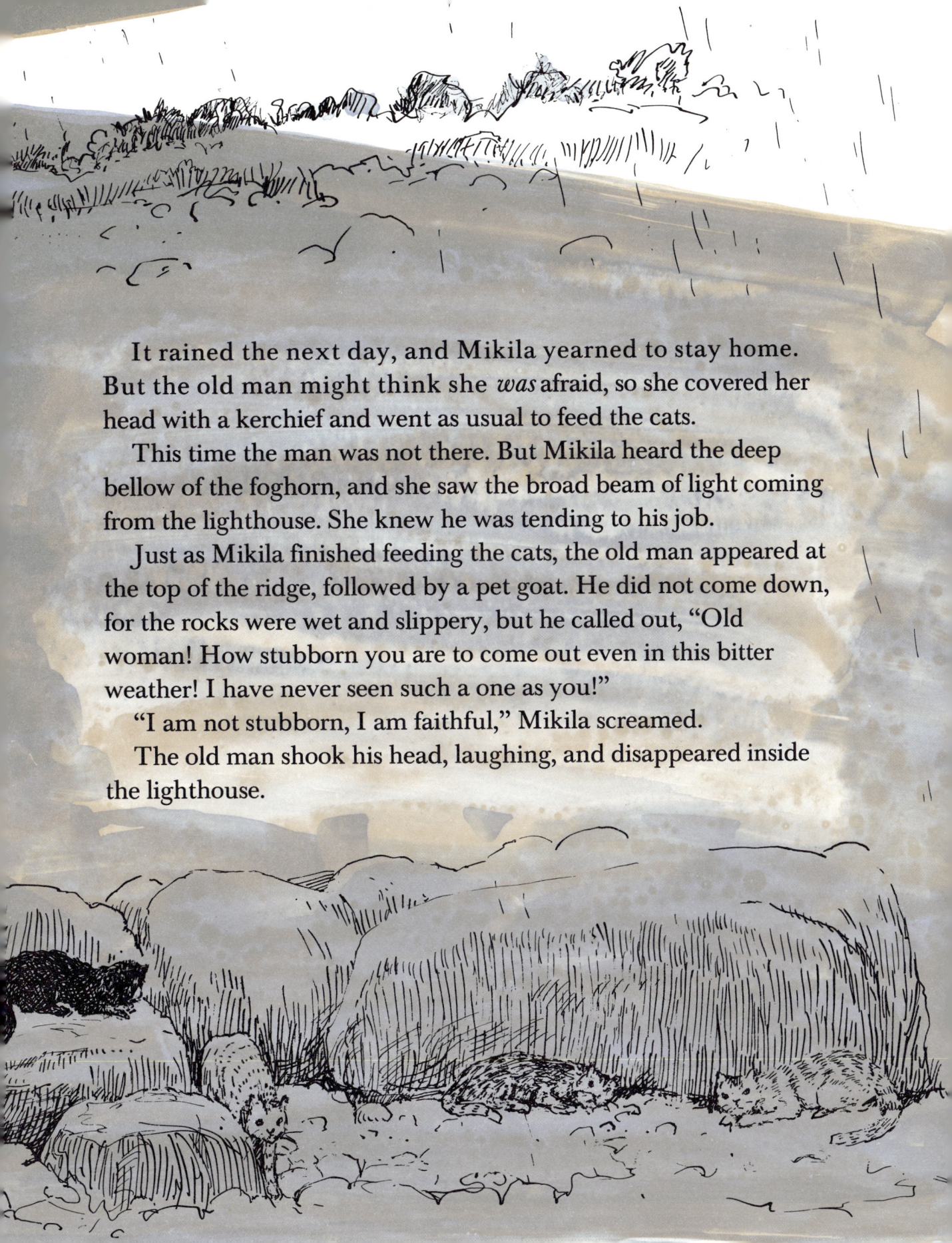

It rained the next day, and Mikila yearned to stay home. But the old man might think she *was* afraid, so she covered her head with a kerchief and went as usual to feed the cats.

This time the man was not there. But Mikila heard the deep bellow of the foghorn, and she saw the broad beam of light coming from the lighthouse. She knew he was tending to his job.

Just as Mikila finished feeding the cats, the old man appeared at the top of the ridge, followed by a pet goat. He did not come down, for the rocks were wet and slippery, but he called out, "Old woman! How stubborn you are to come out even in this bitter weather! I have never seen such a one as you!"

"I am not stubborn, I am faithful," Mikila screamed.

The old man shook his head, laughing, and disappeared inside the lighthouse.

Mikila walked away slowly, her feet sinking into the wet sand. Her clothes clung to her body, and she shivered. At home, a hot bath and a cup of tea did much to restore her spirits, but she felt very tired and soon began to sneeze.

The next morning Mikila's throat was sore. Her head hurt. Today, she thought, she must remain home, indoors. Surely the cats could manage without her for just one day.

Then she remembered the old man's rude laughter and her talk about being faithful.

"One who is faithful," she said to herself, "does not give up so easily." She grunted and groaned all the way down to the shore.

As before, the old man sat upon the rock shelf, and when he saw Mikila, he called down, "Old woman, I have seen you here now these many days. Tell me one thing. *Why* do you feed these cats?"

"BECAUSE THEY ARE HUNGRY!" Mikila shouted.

"Hungry! Hungry!" The man's beard shook, and he held his sides with laughter. "Hungry! Ha-ha-ha. That's a good one! Don't you know there are millions of hungry cats in the world? Can you feed all the cats in the world?"

Mikila did not answer. Wearily she gathered up her empty sack and went home, weeping.

That night Mikila's bones ached. Even hot tea did not help. For three days and nights she lay sick with fever. The old man's words echoed in her head: "Woman, you are wasteful and stubborn and foolish." She thought, "It is true. I can never feed all the hungry cats in the world. I am tired and sick. Most of all, I am sick and tired of being taunted by that terrible old man. I will go no more to feed the cats." She lay in her bed, grieving.

At last Mikila slept deeply, and on the fourth morning she woke up feeling strong—not only strong but determined; not only determined but angry!

She got up in haste, pulled on her clothes, snatched up her sack, and hurried to the stores to gather food for the cats.

As she hustled, Mikila planned what she would tell that rude old man. *He* was the foolish one, the stubborn one, the stupid one. Couldn't he see that what *he* did every day in his lighthouse was exactly the same as feeding the cats?

She could hardly wait to catch him on the ledge and shout up, "Why do you bother to send a beam from your lighthouse? You cannot save every ship in the ocean. You cannot guide them all safely to shore. Why do you even try?"

As Mikila picked her way down the rocky path, she called, "Come, Tiger, Mittens, Freckles, Puff. Oh, my poor little ones. Mikila is here. Roscoe, Tinka, and Tabby! Come, Mikila will not fail you."

She expected to see them shivering, half dead from hunger. But instead the cats leaped nimbly out, playfully rubbing against Mikila's legs.

"Ah, my dear ones," Mikila exclaimed, "how I have missed you! But—you look well fed. How can it be?"

Now Mikila saw the old man's goat licking salt from the rocks, and in the next moment there was the old man himself. He stood bent toward the shyest of the cats, feeding it from a sack of liver, fish scraps, and crusts.

"What are you doing?" cried Mikila in surprise.

He turned and stammered, "I—why—I—what does it look like to you, old woman?"

Mikila stared at him until his face grew very red and he looked away out to sea.

"Are you so rich," she taunted, "that you have money to waste on these filthy creatures?"

The old man shuffled his feet.

Mikila folded her arms and asked, "Aren't you afraid you will fall and break your legs on the rocks?"

The old man shook his head and pulled at a thread on his sleeve.

At last Mikila thrust out her chin and bent toward him, shouting, "Why do you come out in this bitter weather? What a foolish man you are!"

The old man smiled slyly while the cats milled about his feet. "Actually," he said, "it was not my idea."

"Then whose?" asked Mikila, tapping her foot.

"My goat's. Ulysses'. He dragged me down here. The cats were making a terrible racket. What else could I do?"

"You could have stayed in your lighthouse," said Mikila.

"But Ulysses is very stubborn," replied the man. "He is also strong and clever. In fact," said the man with a grin, "he is in many ways like you."

"Like me?" Mikila tossed her head. "Many thanks for comparing me to a goat!"

"But this goat," said the man earnestly, "is my good friend." He patted the goat's head with its stubby horns and stiff hair. "We have many conversations, Ulysses and I."

"Then Ulysses must have told you," said Mikila dryly, "that you cannot possibly feed all the cats in the world."

The old man grinned broadly, and his face creased into a thousand wrinkles. "Of course," he replied. "We all know that. But I can at least feed these close at hand. It is much the same," he added, "as tending the lighthouse."

 Mikila was silent for a long moment. Then she smiled. "Since Ulysses cares so much about the cats," she said, "bring him to me tomorrow. I will show him which shops sell the very best scraps."

 "A fine idea," exclaimed the old man. "But Ulysses goes nowhere without me. We shall come together." He turned and, imitating Mikila's own high voice, said, "Good-bye now. Roscoe, Tiger, and Puff. See you tomorrow!"

And so each day after that the man and the woman and the goat went together to buy the scraps and feed the cats—not all the cats in the world, but the ones that lived among the rocks in the shadow of the old lighthouse. And in so doing, Mikila and the old man became the very best of friends. You can see them walking up the rocky path together, talking and laughing as good friends do.